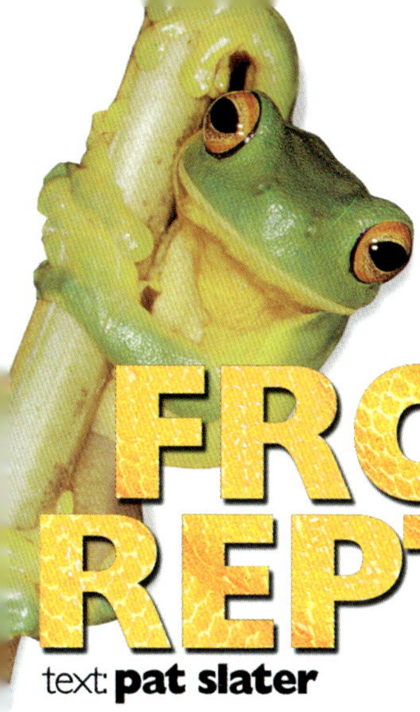

first field guide
to australian
FROGS &
REPTILES

text: **pat slater**

search &learn

Steve Parish
DISCOVER & LEARN
ABOUT AUSTRALIA

Contents

p. 27

FROGS

p. 22

REPTILES

p. 17

p. 29

p. 41

p. 39

An introduction to frogs & reptiles

Frogs and reptiles are vertebrate⁶ animals, whose spinal cords are protected by backbones.

They are ectothermic⁶ (meaning "outside heat") animals, whose bodies are as warm or as cold as their surroundings.

This guide will introduce you to the differences between frogs and reptiles, and help you to recognise the different sorts of reptiles. It will profile some of Australia's most interesting frogs and reptiles. After reading about them, you can go on to discover the rest of these remarkable creatures.

p. 40

Home and away

The frogs and reptiles you will see in the wild in this country are nearly all native⁶ to Australia. One important introduced⁶ animal, the Cane Toad*, is included in this book. It is increasing its range⁶.

p. 23

What will I need?

Comfortable clothes and footwear (long trousers and boots for reptile-finding, gumboots for frog-watching). Hat and sunscreen for daytime, insect repellent for dusk to dawn. Notebook. Torch for night frog-spotting. Books about frogs and reptiles.

* Australia has no native toads.

How to discover frogs & reptiles

🐾 Search in your garden. Look in trees and under bushes. Investigate the roofs and rafters of sheds. Where there is water, there should be frogs. Where there are mice, frogs and insects to eat, there could be reptiles.

🐾 Search the bush. Walk, or sit quietly by a creek or lake. Look for tracks in sand, search for burrows. Very carefully lift up pieces of wood or galvanised iron (tilt away from you so any snakes can escape).

🐾 Explore a safe place at night after the first rain of the season. Look for frogs.

🐾 Locate your local amateur reptile or frog enthusiast and show interest. Raise local tadpoles to frogs.

🐾 Go on a journey to see crocodiles, captive or wild, or marine turtles nesting.

🐾 Watch for seasnakes washed up on the beach. Go snorkeling or scuba diving.

🐾 Go to zoos and museums. Visit national parks and wildlife sanctuaries. Look at reptile and frog displays.

Meeting a snake at a zoo

When do I look for frogs and reptiles ?

Frogs are usually active at night, especially in rainy weather. They are most common in damp places. Track them down by locating calling males, using a torch.

The majority of reptiles are most active during daytime. Spot them basking**ᴳ** in the sun in the early morning or late afternoon.

Some reptiles (e.g. crocodiles, geckos and various snakes) are active on warm nights. Look for them where prey exists.

Watching and recording discoveries

It is usually easy to identify a frog or a reptile as a member of a group, e.g., a freshwater turtle. However, narrowing the identification down further may not be possible in the field. If you can gently handle a reptile or frog, check its characteristics, then replace it where it came from. Do not handle live snakes. Remember that you cannot take creatures protected by law home with you for further study.

It may be impossible to examine an animal closely. Look at the animal in the field as best you can (using binoculars if necessary). Sketch the creature in your notebook, and note down its colours and other features. Identify it later, using a field guide or other reference book. Don't neglect fresh road kills – some exciting discoveries have resulted from studying animals killed on the roads.

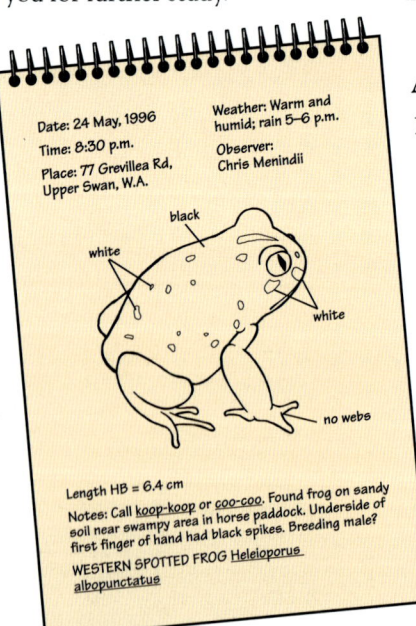

Date: 24 May, 1996
Time: 8:30 p.m.
Place: 77 Grevillea Rd, Upper Swan, W.A.

Weather: Warm and humid; rain 5–6 p.m.
Observer: Chris Menindii

black
white
white
no webs

Length HB = 6.4 cm
Notes: Call koop-koop or coo-coo. Found frog on sandy soil near swampy area in horse paddock. Underside of first finger of hand had black spikes. Breeding male?
WESTERN SPOTTED FROG Heleioporus albopunctatus

Abbreviations

HB = length of head + body to vent
T = length of tail from vent to tip
HBT = head + body + tail
W = weight
♀ = female ♂ = male
Aust. = mainland Australia
Tas. = Tasmania
Vic. = Victoria
NSW = New South Wales
WA = Western Australia
SA = South Australia
NT = Northern Territory
ᴳ = Glossary (p. 56)

6

Naming and grouping animals

An animal may be given **an official common name**, e.g., Thorny Devil, and **unofficial local names**, e.g., Mountain Devil, Moloch.

It is always given **a specific, or scientific, name,** e.g., *Moloch horridus*, which is printed in italics.

A **species**[G] is a group of animals which can breed together to produce fertile[G] offspring. Scientists study material in the body cells of two animals to decide whether or not they are the same species. Frogs give another clue as to their identity – females respond only to the breeding calls of males of their own species.

Species which have similar characteristics are grouped into **genera** (singular = **genus**). Genera are then grouped into **families**. So the Thorny Devil is classified as family Agamidae, genus *Moloch*, species *horridus*.

JIRI LOCHMAN

p. 41

A short history

Frogs and reptiles share common ancestors, the early amphibians[G], which crawled from the seas towards the end of the Devonian Period of Earth's history, around 370 million years ago. A group of these amphibians developed into reptiles, which became the dominant animal group on earth. However, by 65 million years ago, the majority of reptiles were extinct[G], leaving only four major groups to continue on to today (see p. 24).

The skeleton of the dinosaur *Muttaburrasaurus*

QUEENSLAND MUSEUM

Is it a frog or a reptile?

A FROG	A REPTILE
Egg emerges in jelly	Egg has tough shell
Egg laid in moisture	Egg laid in warm, dry place
Egg fertilised[G] outside female's body	Egg fertilised inside female's body
Tadpole (larva) hatches from egg	Small version of adult hatches from egg
Tadpole undergoes big changes to become adult	Reptile grows larger and matures
Frog has moist, glandular[G] skin	Reptile has dry skin from which grow scales
Frog has no tail, 4 limbs	Reptile has tail, may have 4, 2 or no visible limbs
Frog breathes through lungs, inside of mouth, skin	Reptile usually breathes through lungs, or, rarely, skin
Frogs eat insects and other animals	Reptiles usually eat animals, but a few eat plants

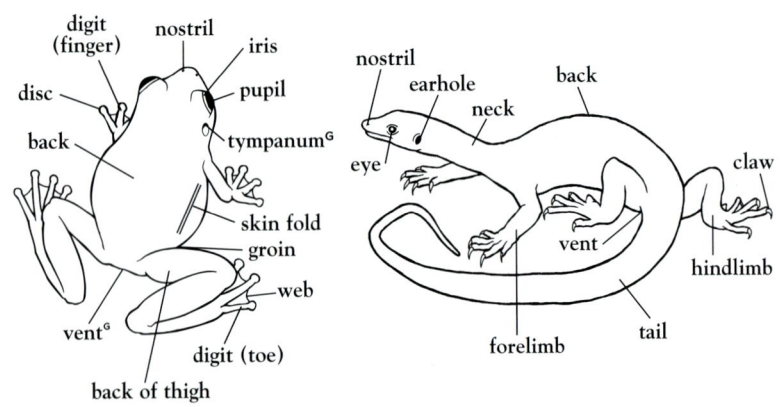

Frog: digit (finger), nostril, iris, pupil, tympanum[G], disc, back, skin fold, groin, web, vent[G], digit (toe), back of thigh

Reptile: nostril, earhole, neck, back, eye, claw, vent, hindlimb, forelimb, tail

Identifying frogs and reptiles

There are many excellent books on groups of Australian animals, including frogs and reptiles.

When trying to identify an animal, it is usually easy to narrow down the possibilities from the maps and photos in a book. To identify the animal's family or its species, most books offer "keys".

A key is a list of paired descriptions, numbered in sequence from 1 onwards. To identify an animal, read the first pair of descriptions (1) and look at the animal. One or the other description will apply to it. On the right hand side of that description will be either the animal's name or a number. If the answer is a number, go on to the pair of descriptions bearing that number. Choose the one which fits the animal. It will lead to either the animal's name or another number (in which case repeat the process).

Eventually you will have a name for your animal.

A simple key to identify the first five frog species in this book:

1	Tips of digits with large discs	**2**
	Tips of digits with small discs	**Striped Rocket-frog**
2	Colour of back green	**3**
	Colour of back not green	**4**
3	Colour of iris orange-red	**Red-eyed Green Tree-frog**
	Colour of iris gold	**Green Tree-frog**
4	Colour of back grey to red-brown, groin yellow	**Naked (Red) Tree-frog**
	Colour of back brown, groin and thigh red	**Blue Mountains Tree-frog**

Green Tree-frog

Litoria caerulea (= blue* beach-frog)

Length: ♀ 6–11; ♂ 6.6–7.7 cm

Identification: Large (cricket-ball-sized) tree-frog with smooth green to green-brown skin on back and sides, sometimes spotted white. Underside is white, with coarsely grainy texture. Back of thigh is yellow to maroon. Pupil horizontal[G], iris pale yellow to gold. Large glands on back of head. Fold of skin overhangs tympanum. Digits end in large discs. Fingers are $^1/_3$ webbed, toes $^3/_4$ webbed.

Where found: Across northern half of Aust. In moist, cool places, in both natural situations and human constructions such as toilets and drainpipes.

Call: Deep, repeated *crawk…crawk*.

Habits: Spends daytime in moist refuge, hunts small creatures at night. Active climber. Lays 200–2000 eggs after rain falls (Nov.–Feb.). Mottled brown or green tadpoles grow 4.5–10.0 cm, take about 6 weeks to mature to frogs.

Notes: Becomes very used to humans. If removed from refuge tends to return. Less active in cold, dry weather, begins calling when rain falls.

Status[G]: Secure.

Similar species: Magnificent Tree-frog, *L. splendida*, has gland covering entire head. White-lipped Tree-frog, *L. infrafrenata*, has white stripe around edge of lower jaw.

* Named after a dead frog preserved in alcohol, which turned it blue.

HABITAT
MOIST
PLACES

FOOD
INSECTS &
SMALL LIFE

Red-eyed Green Tree-frog

Litoria chloris (= green beach-frog)

Length: ♀ 5.8–6.8; ♂ 5.4–6.2 cm

Identification: Medium (tennis-ball-sized) tree-frog with smooth, bright green back and white to bright yellow, grainy underside. Back of thigh is purple or brown. Pupil is horizontal, iris is gold in centre, orange or red at edge. Digits end in large discs. Fingers are $^3/4$ webbed, toes are $^7/8$ webbed.

Where found: Coastal wet forests and regrowth around clearings, along northern NSW coast and Qld coast, as far north as Proserpine.

Call: Repeated, long, moaning *aaa-rk…aaa-rk,* followed by soft trill.

Habits: Lives in foliage high in trees. After heavy rain, usually Oct.–Feb., calls from lower branches. Large groups gather around flooded areas and overflow ponds to breed. Eggs laid singly or in clumps in shallow water. Pale brown tadpoles grow to 7.4 cm.

Notes: Because of their treetop habitat, these frogs are usually seen only after heavy rain falls and they come to the ground to breed.

Status: Secure.

Similar species: Orange-thighed Frog, *L. xanthomera,* found north of Proserpine, Qld, has orange at back of thigh.

IAN MORRIS

HABITAT
COASTAL
FORESTS

FOOD
INSECTS &
SMALL LIFE

Naked (Red) Tree-frog

Litoria rubella (= red beach-frog)

Length: ♀ 3.4–4.3; ♂ 2.8–3.7 cm

Identification: Small (ping-pong-ball-sized) stocky tree-frog with smooth, pale grey to reddish-brown back, with small darker flecks. Dark stripe along side of head and body. Underside is white and grainy (throat of breeding male is dark grey). Groin is yellow. Pupil is horizontal, iris is gold. Limbs are short; digits have large discs; fingers are slightly webbed, toes $^2/_3$ webbed.

Call: Long, pulsing note, rising towards end.

Where found: Northern $^3/_4$ of Aust. Absent from southern coastal areas.

Habits: Spends day sheltering under stone or bark, sometimes in a building or under a water pipe. Breeds straight after heavy rain. Males call from ground near water. Thin layer of up to 300 eggs floats on surface. Tadpole is pale brown and grows to 3.9 cm.

Notes: Found in both arid and wet coastal areas. Breeding time varies according to rain.

Status: Secure.

Similar species: Buzzing Tree-frog, *L. electrica*, around Gulf of Carpentaria. Bleating Tree-frog, *L. dentata*, in coastal southern Qld and northern to central NSW. Both have large, dark markings on their backs.

JIRI LOCHMAN

HABITAT
PLAINS &
FORESTS

FOOD
INSECTS &
SMALL LIFE

Blue Mountains Tree-frog

Litoria citropa (= lemon-coloured beach-frog)

Length: ♀ 5.6–5.7; ♂ 4.7–5.7 cm

Identification: Medium-sized tree-frog. Smooth skin on the top of the head and back is light to dark brown, flecked or mottled black. Green on side of head, on flank and on limbs. Black line from nostril through eye over tympanum to groin. Side, groin, inner and outer thigh are orange-red. Pupil is horizontal, iris is gold. Digits have large discs. Fingers lack webbing, toes are half-webbed.

Call: A scream, followed by a soft trill.

Where found: Flowing streams in rocky, forested areas, from the Great Dividing Range to the coast in NSW and eastern Vic.

Habits: Rarely seen unless the determined frog-watcher searches the preferred habitat of rocky outcrops. Males call in Sept. and Oct., usually from near fast-flowing water.

Eggs may be found on rocks or in pools in streams. Tadpole is dark brown marked with gold, grows to 3.4 cm.

Notes: Described as Australia's most beautiful frog, and featured on a postage stamp.

Status: Secure.

Similar species: None.

IAN MORRIS

HABITAT
STREAMS,
FORESTS

FOOD
INSECTS &
SMALL LIFE

Striped Rocket-frog

Litoria nasuta (= large-nosed beach-frog)

Length: ♀ 3.6–5.5; ♂ 3.3–4.5 cm

Identification: Medium-sized, streamlined frog with a long snout, long arms and very long, powerful legs. Centre of back pale brown, bordered by darker brown areas, marked with still darker bumps. Skin folds run down back. Black and white stripes from nose along side to flank. Underside is white and grainy. Back of thigh is yellow with dark brown stripes. Tympanum has white border. Discs on digits are small. No webs between fingers.

Call: *Wick–wick–wick…but…but…but.*

Where found: Coastal waterways and swamps, from north of Newcastle, NSW, to Cape York Peninsula, and across NT to Kimberley, WA.

Habits: Lives on ground, hunts at night. Breeds between Nov. and Feb. in northern Aust. Groups of 50–100 eggs float on surface of water. Tadpoles are mottled with brown above and may grow to 5.6 cm.

Notes: This frog is a fast, strong leaper.

Status: Secure.

Similar species: Freycinet's Frog, *L. freycineti,* found in northeastern NSW and southwest Qld, also has long hindlegs, but has rows of warts rather than narrow skin folds on its back.

HABITAT SWAMPS & WATERWAYS

FOOD INSECTS & SMALL LIFE

Water-holding Frog

Cyclorana platycephala (= flat-headed round-frog)

Length: ♀ 5.0–7.2;
♂ 4.2–6.4 cm

Identification: Medium-sized, round-bodied, short-legged frog. Dull grey, brown or green back, sometimes marked with pale stripe down centre and darker patches. Head flattened, and tympanum much larger than eye.

PETER SLATER

Small eye set high on head, has horizontal pupil, gold iris. No webs on fingers, but toes are fully webbed. Shovel-shaped tubercle^G on inner side of foot.

Call: Repeated, lengthy *maw-w..maw-w-w*.

Where found: Inland arid areas of all Aust. except Vic., near waterholes and swamps which fill after rain.

Habits: In dry conditions, uses sharp-edged tubercle on foot to dig burrow at foot of bush or tree and aestivates^G. Frog's outer layer of skin forms a water-saving cocoon, its bladder serves as storage tank for water in form of very dilute urine. After rain falls, frog surfaces, sheds and eats cocoon, feeds and breeds.

Notes: Two separated groups (see map). Can capture food in water, and webbed feet make it a good swimmer. Used as water source by humans.

Status: Secure.

Similar species: No other burrowing frog has a flattened head, small eyes, no eye-stripe and fully webbed toes.

HABITAT
INLAND
ARID AREAS

FOOD
INSECTS &
SMALL LIFE

Northern Snapping (Giant) Frog

Cyclorana australis (= southern round-frog)

IAN MORRIS

Length: ♀ 7.1–10.5; ♂ 7.1–7.9 cm

Identification: A large, burrowing frog with a large, flattish, broad head and very large eyes. Skin of back bumpy and may be pale brown, grey or green, with dark markings or green patches. Broad, dark stripe from tip of nose to flank. One skin fold runs down each side of the backbone, another on each side to the flank. Pupil is horizontal, iris gold. Back of thigh is patterned. Fingers are unwebbed, toes have small webs. A shovel-shaped tubercle on inner side of foot.

Call: Short, repeated *unk...unk...unk.*

Where found: Open forest and grassland across northern Australia, from Broome to western side of the base of Cape York Peninsula.

Habits: Often seen during the Wet season, sometimes basking in hot sunshine beside water. During Dry remains in burrow. Breeds in Wet, between Dec. and Feb., laying up to 7000 eggs in temporary water. Creamy gold tadpoles grow to 7.0 cm and swim in large groups.

Notes: Has a tremendous gape[G] and will eat any creature small enough to swallow, including other frogs.

Status: Secure.

Similar species: New Holland Frog, *C. novaehollandiae*, which lacks the pattern on the back of the thigh, replaces this frog in most of Queensland.

HABITAT
FLOODED
GRASSLAND

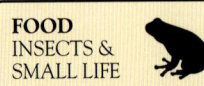

FOOD
INSECTS &
SMALL LIFE

Northern Banjo Frog

Limnodynastes terraereginae (= Queensland lord-of-the-marshes)

Length: ♀ 5.5–7.9; ♂ 6.0–7.6 cm

Identification: A large, burrowing frog. The bumpy skin of the back is brown or black, with darker markings and a paler central stripe. The underside is cream, the side yellow with black markings, the groin yellow and scarlet. The male displays a yellow throat sac. A yellow gland runs from beneath the eye back to the shoulder. Horizontal pupil, gold iris. Digits have no discs. Toes have small webs.

Call: Repeated *plonk…plonk… plonk* like plucking a banjo.

Where found: Vegetation near still water, in woodlands and forests in coastal eastern Aust. Some inland range in NSW.

Habits: Found near permanent water. Hides in grass or other vegetation during day. After rain, from Oct. to May, breeding males call from water. Tadpoles reach 6.5 cm, have dark bodies and mottled tails.

Notes: As female lays eggs, she paddles with her broad inner fingers. Air bubbles pass under her body, mingle with the eggs and jelly coming from her vent and form a floating foam nest.

Status: Secure.

Similar species: Pobblebonk, *L. dorsalis*, in southwestern WA. Giant Bullfrog, *L. interioris*, of drier areas NSW and Vic. lacks scarlet in groin.

HABITAT PLANTS NEAR WATER

FOOD INSECTS & SMALL LIFE

Southern Gastric-brooding Frog

Rheobatrachus silus (= pug-nosed stream-frog)

Length: ♀ 4.5–5.4; ♂ 3.3–4.1 cm

Identification: Medium-sized, water-dwelling, short-snouted frog with slimy skin and large, powerful hindlegs. Bumpy back varies from brown to greenish, with darker patches. Underside white with patches of yellow. The large eyes, which have vertical[G] pupils, are set on top of the head. Fingers are unwebbed, toes fully webbed.

Call: A rising note.

Where found: In rocky rainforest streams and pools above 300 m altitude[G], in the Conondale and Blackall Ranges, southeastern Qld.

Habits: Lives in water, and is active at night. A female swallows up to 25 fertilised eggs (or possibly tadpoles), which develop to adult frogs in her stomach. After around 6 weeks, small frogs emerge from their mother's mouth; she then begins feeding again.

Notes: May be seen drifting in water, or floating on its back. Tongue cannot be flicked out of mouth, so probably gulps insects from water. This remarkable frog has not been seen since 1981.

Status: May be extinct.

Similar species: Larger (♀ 6.6–7.9 mm) Northern Gastric-brooding Frog, *R. vitellinus*, of Clarke Range, near Mackay, Qld, not seen since 1985.

OWEN KELLY

HABITAT RAINFOREST STREAMS

FOOD INSECTS & WATER LIFE

Adelotus brevis (= short unseen frog)

Length: ♀ 2.9–3.8; ♂ 3.4–3.8 mm

IAN MORRIS

Identification: Small, large-headed, flattened frog. Skin on back is rough with warts and ridges, and is grey or brown, patterned darker. Throat grey with white flecks, belly smooth and black with white spots (males) or marbling (females). Both sexes have tusk-like teeth at front of lower jaw. Bright red patches in groin and on back of hindleg.

Call: *Kuruk*, repeated several times a minute.

Where found: In forest and open country, on the coastal plain and in the Great Dividing Range, from central eastern Qld to southern NSW.

Habits: Lives under rocks or logs, or in crevices, near water. Pale cream eggs are laid in a foam nest, usually away from direct light. Male remains with nest until tadpoles hatch.

Notes: Male is larger than female (not usual in frogs) and male head is wider than (and may be same size as) its body. The tusks are used in fights between males.

Status: Secure.

Similar species: No other frog has such a large head and tusks.

HABITAT
FORESTS & PLAINS

FOOD
INSECTS & SMALL LIFE

Western Spotted Frog

Heleioporus albopunctatus (= white-spotted marsh-dweller)

JIRI LOCHMAN

Call: Repeated short, high *coo…coo*.

Where found: In sandy country, usually near water, in the southwest of WA, except southwestern corner.

Habits: Males call from the mouths of their burrows, females search them out. 250–700 eggs are deposited and fertilised to form a frothy mass. Hatching takes place after the burrow is flooded by rain.

Length: ♀ 6.0–8.5; ♂ 5.6–7.7 cm

Identification: Large, fat, burrowing frog, with a broad, rounded head. Back and sides are leather-textured and dark brown to black, spotted with white or yellow. The underside is white. A white stripe runs from front of eye to snout and another from bottom of eye to hinge of mouth. The pupil is vertical. Digits are unwebbed, toes short. Foot has a large digging tubercle on its inner side. Breeding male has black spines on the first finger.

Notes: Seen on the surface on summer and autumn nights. Calling begins with winter rains in April or May. To locate a calling male, find the entrance to his burrow.

Status: Not common.

Similar species: Other *Heleioporus* species found in southwestern WA lack white or yellow spots on the back.

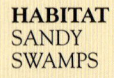
HABITAT
SANDY
SWAMPS

FOOD
INSECTS &
SMALL LIFE

Desert Spadefoot Frog

Notaden nichollsi (= Nicholls's back-gland*)

Length: ♀ 4.6–6.5;
♂ 4.2–5.8 cm

Identification: Small, fat, short-legged frog with a short head and bumpy skin. The back is green-grey to brown, spotted with yellow and red warts, while the underside is pale. The tympanum is not obvious. The eye has a horizontal pupil. The fingers are unwebbed, the toes are slightly webbed.

IAN MORRIS

Call: A loud *woop…woop…woop.*

Where found: In aridland and grassland, from northwestern WA across to southwestern Qld and south to northern SA.

Habits: During drought aestivates at end of burrow sunk up to 2 m into ground. With rain, comes to surface, feeds on ants and termites.

Males call while floating in water. Up to 1000 eggs laid in a chain in flooded vegetation. Pale brown tadpoles may become frogs in only 16 days.

Notes: One of four *Notaden* species which can survive long dry periods in their burrow then breed in temporary flooding after rain falls. Runs rather than hops.

Status: Secure.

Similar species: No other *Notaden* species in its range.

* *Notaden* frogs have skin glands which "sweat" a distasteful substance.

HABITAT
ARID
COUNTRY

FOOD
ANTS &
TERMITES

Australian Freshwater Crocodile

Crocodylus johnstoni (= Johnstone's crocodile)

Length: HBT up to 3 m

Identification: Comparatively slender crocodile. Upper surface grey to green-brown with darker markings. Underside is whitish. Snout is long, slender and smooth; teeth are slender and sharp.

Where found: Permanent fresh water (billabongs, swamps, rivers) in northern and northeastern Aust. Occasionally in tidal waters, or walking overland at night between bodies of water.

Habits: Found where plants or rocks overhang water. Basks on banks or in shallow water, but spends most of its time in the water. From sunset, hunts small animals, including insects, fish, frogs, birds and reptiles, in the water. Female lays 12–20 eggs in a nest in a sandbank towards end of Dry season (Oct.–Nov.). A female (may not be mother) digs out the nest when young hatch, and may carry them to water in her mouth.

Notes: Not harmful to humans. However, will bite if seized or interfered with.

Status: Secure.

Similar species: Small Saltwater Crocodile has broad, bumpy snout.

HABITAT SWAMPS & RIVERS

FOOD MAINLY WATER LIFE

Saltwater (Estuarine) Crocodile

Crocodylus porosus (= pore-skinned crocodile)

Length: HBT up to 7 m

Identification: Small to enormous crocodile. Upper surface brown, grey or nearly black with dark markings. Underside whitish. Snout short in comparison to width, broad and has grainy, bumpy surface.

Where found: Sea, estuaries, swamps, rivers and floodplains in northern Aust.

Habits: Basks or shelters in shade along banks during day, hunts animals in or near water at night. Large male holds a territory⁶. Female mates early in Wet season, lays up to 60 hard-shelled eggs in nest of vegetation on river bank. She later cares for the hatchlings.

Notes: A potential danger to humans. Numbers recovering since hunting stopped in 1970s.

Status: Secure.

Similar species: Freshwater Crocodile has slender snout.

HABITAT FRESH & SALT WATER

FOOD LAND OR WATER LIFE

What sort of turtle is it?

A key to the families of Australian turtles:

1   Limbs like paddles, without joints
or clawed, webbed feet **2**

    Limbs have joints and webbed,
clawed feet...**freshwater turtles**
(about 22 species, examples pp. 29, 30)

2   Nostrils set at end
of a fleshy snout ....**Pig-nosed Turtle**
(1 species, not described in this book, photo above)

    Nostrils set level with surface of nose **3**

3   Paddle-like limbs have claws...............................**sea turtles**
(6 species, examples pp. 31, 32)

    Paddle-like limbs have no claws.........**Leatherback Turtle**
(1 species, not described in this book, photo below)

Leatherback Turtle

Eastern Snake-necked Turtle

Chelodina longicollis (= long-necked little tortoise)

Length: Carapace to 25 cm

Identification: Dinner-plate-sized, long-necked freshwater turtle with head plus neck measurement as long as, or longer than, shell length. Carapace brown or black, with black seams between its plates. Head flattened, eyes look sideways, nostrils on tip of snout. Front foot webbed, with 4 clawed digits.

Where found: Coastal and inland wetlands and rivers, from eastern Qld to southeastern SA.

Habits: Basks on sandbank or submerged log. Feeds on animals found in water. In summer, may wander in search of water, or burrow into mud and aestivate.

Female lays 12 or more brittle-shelled eggs in hole in earth bank in early summer. Hatchlings emerge up to 5 months later, after rain has dampened nest.

Notes: When underwater, pushes nostrils above surface in order to breathe.

Status: Secure.

Similar species: Very large Broad-shelled Snake-necked Turtle, *C. expansa*, found in Murray-Darling River system and coastal central Qld.

HABITAT
RIVERS &
WETLANDS

FOOD
WATER &
OTHER LIFE

Western Swamp Turtle

Pseudemydura umbrina (= shaded false *Emydura**)

JIRI LOCHMAN

Length: Carapace to 15 cm

Identification: Saucer-sized, short-necked, freshwater turtle. Brown carapace is almost square in outline. Plastron pale with dark seams between plates. Head and neck much shorter than shell; head broad and flat and protected by horny shield. Front feet webbed with 5 clawed digits.

Where found: One small swamp at Ellenbrook, north of Perth, WA.

Habits: Lives in an area of summer drought and winter rain. Spends 6–9 months of each year aestivating under soil or in ground litter. Becomes active when its habitat is flooded with water, which needs to be above 14°C in temperature.

Notes: A hatchling needs to grow for 2 seasons before aestivating successfully. It may not breed until over 15 years of age. This is Australia's rarest reptile, which needs protection. A captive breeding program is under way.

Status: Rare and endangered.

Similar species: None.

* Emydura is another genus of short-necked turtles.

HABITAT
PAPERBARK
SWAMP

FOOD
WATER
LIFE

Loggerhead Turtle

Caretta caretta (= tortoise-shell turtle)

Length: Carapace to 1.5 m

Identification: Large to enormous sea turtle, with dark reddish-brown carapace, speckled darker, and pale plastron. Adult head is massive, jaws powerful and flippers small (compared with heads and flippers of other sea turtle species).

Where found: Tropical and warm temperate waters around northern Aust.

Habits: Feeds on molluscs, crabs, sea urchins (helped by large jaw muscles) and sea jellies. Female mates in sea, then lays up to 125 eggs in a pit dug above high tide mark. After 60–80 days, hatchlings dig from nest at night and make their way to the sea.

Notes: One of the 4 species of sea turtle which nests regularly along Qld coast. Main South Pacific nest site is on Wreck Island, in the Capricorn Bunker Group, Qld; mainland nest site is at Mon Repos, near Bundaberg, Qld. Hatchlings are reddish-brown above, dark blackish-brown below.

Status: Rare and endangered.

Similar species: No other sea turtle has such a massive head.

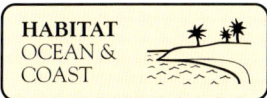
HABITAT OCEAN & COAST

FOOD MOLLUSCS & SEA LIFE

Green Turtle

Chelonia mydas (= *mydas* tortoise*)

Length: Carapace up to 1 m

Identification: Large sea turtle with an olive-green, high-domed carapace mottled with darker brown and black, and a pale plastron. Shell may be oval or almost heart-shaped. Head of an adult is small in relation to its body size.

Where found: Coral reefs and seagrass flats, in tropical and warm temperate waters along northern coasts of Aust.

Habits: Feeds on seaweeds and seagrasses. May return 1000 km to nest site. Female mates in water and may explore a beach before digging a hole above high tide mark and laying up to 200 soft-shelled eggs in it. More clutches laid at intervals of up to 15 days. Eggs hatch in 54–70 days.

Notes: This is the only vegetarian turtle and it is a traditional human food. Outside Aust., flesh and eggs eaten, shell used for jewellery, skin for leather, oil for cosmetics. In danger from fishing nets, powerboats.

Status: Decreasing in numbers.

Similar species: None.

* Meaning of mydas unknown.

HABITAT OCEANS & COASTS

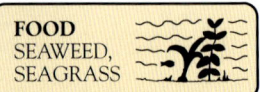
FOOD SEAWEED, SEAGRASS

What sort of lizard is it?

A key to the families of Australian lizards:

1 Eyes either with movable lids or without movable lids
   Has limbs (which may be small) **2**
   Has no limbs; there may be a scaly flap instead **5**

2 Eyes with or without movable lids.
   Pupil is not a vertical slit in daylight.
   Scales on head and neck are overlapping **3**

   Eyes without movable lids.
   Pupil is a vertical slit in daylight.
   Scales on head and neck lie side by side ....**geckos**
               (over 100 Australian species, examples pp. 34, 35)

3 Scales on the top of the head are tiny and irregular **4**
   Scales on the top of the head are large, regular
   and shield-like ....**skinks**
               (over 300 Australian species, examples pp. 36, 37)

4 Tongue is long, slender, deeply forked, often flickered
   in and out when owner is alert ....**monitors**
               (over 25 Australian species, examples pp. 38, 39)

   Tongue is broad and flat with a small notch in front.
   Appears when owner eats and drinks ....**dragons**
               (over 60 Australian species, examples pp. 40, 41)

5 Eyes are without movable eyelids ....**legless lizards**
               (over 30 Australian species, examples pp. 42, 43)

   Eyes have eyelids...**some skinks**

Variegated Dtella

Gehyra variegata (= variegated *Gehyra**)

Length: HB to 5.5 cm; T to 7cm

Identification: Medium-sized, soft-skinned gecko with flattened body and depression at base of tail. Upper surface grey or grey-brown with many darker markings. Underside whitish. Lidless eye has a vertical pupil. Digits expanded into large pads; all but the innermost bear claws.

Where found: From coastal WA (except southwestern corner and Kimberley) across interior of Aust.

Habits: Spends the day under loose bark or in a tree hollow, under a rock flake or in a crevice of a building. At night roams sloping and vertical surfaces, hunting insects and spiders. Female lays 1 egg, often in a nest with other females' eggs.

Notes: Changes colour from darker during day to paler at night. Able to lose tail and later regrow it. Cleans eyes with tongue. Several may share a daytime shelter.

Status: Secure.

Similar species: Dubious Dtella, *G. dubia*, in coastal Qld and northern NSW; Top-end Dtella, *G. australis*, in northern NT, WA.

* Meaning of *Gehyra* is unknown.

IAN MORRIS

HABITAT TREES, ROCKS & HOUSES

FOOD INSECTS, SPIDERS

Three-lined Knob-tailed Gecko

Nephrurus levis (= smooth kidney-tail)

JIRI LOCHMAN

Length: HB to 9 cm; T to 5.4 cm

Identification: Large, big-headed gecko with a short, fat tail ending in a small knob. Upper surface purple-brown with white tubercles in lines. Yellowish bars across head, neck and shoulder. Underside white. Digits end in claws.

Where found: In dry, sandy country, open woodland and grassland from central coast of WA to arid interiors of all mainland States except Vic.

Habits: Shelters during day and in cold weather in a tunnel it has dug in the side of another animal's burrow, or in its own burrow. At night, hunts insects, spiders, scorpions and other geckos. Remains able to run fast when cold slows other lizards.

Notes: Knobbed tail vibrated and twitched in alarm or aggression. Tail not easily shed.

Status: Secure.

Similar species: Smooth Knob-tail Gecko, *N. laevissimus*, has dark bars across head, neck and upper back.

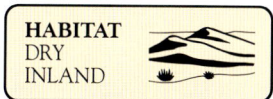
HABITAT
DRY
INLAND

FOOD
SMALL LIFE,
GECKOS

Shingleback (Lizard)

Trachydosaurus rugosus (= wrinkled, rough lizard)

Length: HB to 31 cm; T to 8 cm

Identification: Large, long-bodied, short-tailed skink with enlarged, rough, pine-cone-like scales on upper surface. Has a huge, triangular (from above) head. Tail short, rounded and blunt-ended. Upper surface pale to dark reddish- or yellowish-brown with paler markings. Underside smooth and pale.

Where found: Southern half of Aust., except for eastern and southeastern coastal areas.

Habits: Moves slowly across ground during day, feeding on insects, snails, vegetation (including fungi) and carrion. Shelters under timber, grass or ground litter in cold weather. Mates in spring, 2 or 3 large young born in summer.

Notes: Tail used to store fat. When threatened, shows blue tongue and hisses, but is reluctant to bite.

Status: Secure.

Similar species: Bluetongues have smooth scales on backs.

HABITAT WOODLANDS & PLAINS

FOOD PLANTS & ANIMALS

Common Bluetongue

Tiliqua scincoides (= *Scincus*-like *tiliqua**)

Length: HB to 37 cm; T to 56 cm

Identification: Large, long-bodied skink with smooth scales on upper surface. Upper surface pale grey to brown, with 6–9 darker bands across body and 6–8 across tail, which tapers to a point. Underside smooth and pale.

Where found: From southeastern SA through Vic., eastern NSW and Qld to northern NT and northwestern WA.

Habits: Shelters under timber or litter in colder weather. During day and warm evenings feeds on insects, snails, vegetation and carrion.

Female has live young and may produce up to 25 young at a birth.

Notes: One of the world's largest skinks. Blue tongue shown in defensive warning.

Status: Secure.

Similar species: Centralian Bluetongue, *T. multifasciata*, has 11–13 bands on body; Western Bluetongue, *T. occipitalis*, 5–7.

* After a genus of skinks.

HABITAT
FORESTS &
GRASSLANDS

FOOD
PLANTS &
ANIMALS

Gould's Monitor

Varanus gouldii (= Gould's monitor*)

Length: HB to 65.5 cm; T to 100 cm

Identification: Very large, ground-living monitor. Upper surface varies from yellow to nearly black, with lighter and darker markings which form crossbands. Dark stripe from eye to ear. Eyes have round pupils, eyelids are well developed. Long forked tongue flicks to carry scent to organ in roof of mouth. Limbs are powerful, digits clawed.

Where found: All over Aust. except extreme southeast and in high rainfall forests.

Habits: Shelters in a burrow or log. Hunts smaller animals, eats carrion. During breeding season, males may fight. Female buries up to 11 eggs in a nest dug in earth in spring or summer; hatchlings emerge following spring.

Notes: Tail used as prop, to balance body, or as weapon.

Status: Secure.

Similar species: Perentie, *V. giganteus*, is larger, has rows of spots across upper surface.

* Monitors were thought to watch for crocodiles and warn of their presence.

IAN MORRIS

HABITAT GROUND HABITATS

FOOD CARRION & GROUND LIFE

Lace Monitor

Varanus varius (= several-coloured monitor)

Length: HB to 76.5 cm; T to 134 cm

Identification: Large, tree-living monitor which may hunt on ground. Upper surface dark blue with scattered white or yellow scales forming spots and blotches. Black bars across snout, chin and throat. Tail banded with yellow.

Where found: Forests, woodlands and plains of eastern coast and ranges; along Murray-Darling River system; Flinders Ranges.

Habits: Eats nestling birds as well as other tree-dwelling and ground animals and carrion. Female lays up to 12 eggs in hole in ground or stump or dug into termite mound built in tree or on the ground. She may later return to free the hatchlings (or to dig out nest to lay the following season).

Notes: May frequent picnic grounds, hoping for scraps –

is easy to chase away. Takes refuge in tree, keeping on opposite side of trunk from danger.

Status: Secure.

Similar species: Gould's Goanna *V. gouldii* is ground-dwelling, and its back has yellow background colour rather than dark blue.

HABITAT
WOODLANDS
& PLAINS

FOOD
TREE LIFE
& CARRION

Frilled Lizard

Chlamydosaurus kingii (= King's cloaked lizard)

Length: HB to 28 cm; T to 67 cm

Identification: A large dragon with a frill of skin around head. Upper surface grey to orange-brown, with darker markings. Frill yellow to black, flashing orange or red when opened. Underside pale; male has black belly. Eye has round pupil and movable lids. Limbs are well developed and digits clawed. If broken off, the tail does not grow again.

Where found: In woodlands from Kimberley Division, WA, across top of NT to Cape York Peninsula and eastern Qld.

Habits: Perches on tree trunks and on branches, colour and broken outline acting as camouflage[G]. Moves to keep tree between itself and danger. On ground, may run on hindlimbs. Eats insects and other creatures in trees and on ground. Female lays 8–14 eggs.

Notes: The reptile emblem of Australia. Frill is supported by rods connected to tongue and jaws, so when mouth opens frill spreads, showing orange and red scales.

Status: Not secure.

Similar species: None.

HABITAT WARMER WOODLANDS

FOOD INSECTS & SMALL LIFE

Thorny Devil

Moloch horridus (= bristly devil)

Length: HB to 10 cm; T to 9 cm

Identification: Medium-sized dragon with a flattened body, bumpy, spiky skin and a tiny head. Large two-spined hump on neck. Can slowly change colour and pattern to match the ground it stands on.

Where found: Dry country, from central coast of WA across interior of Aust., including most of SA, to western Qld.

Habits: Moves slowly around in daytime, feeding on small ants (up to 5000 in a meal). Does not drink. Water falling on skin makes its way through series of skin grooves to mouth. Female lays up to 10 eggs in a nest at the end of a long tunnel. Young breed after 3 years, may live to 20 years.

Notes: When threatened, bends head so spiky neck bump becomes a false head.

Status: Secure.

Similar species: None.

HABITAT
ARID
COUNTRY

FOOD
SMALL
BLACK ANTS

What sort of snake is it?

A key to the families of Australian snakes:

1   Tail cylinder-shaped, not flattened..**2**

    Tail flattened and paddle-shaped ....**seasnakes**
(over 30 Australian species, example p. 55)

2   Scales on belly more or less equal in size
      to scales on back and sides...**3**

  One row of scales on belly. Each scale at least
      three times as wide as a scale on back or sides.................**4**

3   Eyes well developed. Body scales rough and keeled.
      More than 80 scales around middle of body ....**file snakes**
(2 Australian species, example p. 47)

  Eyes dark spots beneath scales. Body scales smooth.
      Fewer than 40 scales around middle of body......**blind snakes**
(over 40 Australian species, example p. 48)

4   Fewer than 30 scales around middle of body..........................**5**

  More than 30 scales around middle of body...............**pythons**
(15 Australian species, examples pp. 45, 46)

5   Two scales cover vent ....**colubrid snakes**
(11 Australian species, example p. 49)

  Single scale covers vent ....**elapid snakes**
(75 Australian species, examples pp. 50–54)

Diamond (Carpet) Python

Morelia spilota (= spotted *Morelia*)

Length: HB to 350 cm; T to 50 cm

Identification: Diamond Python subspecies[G] has upper surface green-black, with cream or yellow spots forming diamond pattern (see right). Carpet Python subspecies has upper surface pale to dark brown, with paler blotches, each with dark border forming "carpet" pattern (see below).

Where found: Aust. except southern Vic., arid Centre and northwest.

Habits: Often hunts and shelters in trees, but may hunt on ground and shelter in

burrows of other animals. Eats birds and mammals, killing them by crushing them with its body. Female lays up to 50 eggs, then coils around them until they hatch.

Notes: Tracks prey using heat-sensitive pits on lips. Has no venom and is harmless to humans. Kills rats, mice.

Status: Secure.

Similar snakes: There are 3 subspecies of this python and numbers of other colour forms.

HABITAT TREES & GROUND

FOOD BIRDS & MAMMALS

Black-headed Python

Aspidites melanocephalus (= black-headed shield-bearer)

STANLEY BREEDEN

Length: HB to 265 cm; T to 35 cm

Identification: A large, small-headed, round-snouted python with a glossy black head and neck. Upper surface of body and tail light tan to brown, with many darker cross bands. Eye has vertical pupil. Lips lack heat-sensing pits present in most other pythons.

Where found: Plains and ranges across northern half of Aust.

Habits: Ground-living python which shelters in cracks in soil, burrows, fallen trees, termite mounds and caves. At night, hunts for ground-living birds, mammals and reptiles, including snakes. Lacks venom and kills prey by crushing it in body coils. Males fight in mating season. Female lays 5–9 eggs, coils round them and may warm them by shivering.

Notes: During cool weather, black head is pushed into sunlight and warms rapidly.

Status: Secure.

Similar species: Woma Python, *A. ramsayi*, of drier central Aust., the other python without lip pits, lacks black head colour.

HABITAT
PLAINS &
RANGES

FOOD
REPTILES &
OTHER LIFE

Arafura File Snake

Acrochordus arafurae (= Arafura* pointed-scale)

Length: HBT to 164 cm

Identification: Large, water-living snake with small head and loose skin. Upper surface grey to dark brown, marked with pale blotches. Scales small, keeled and resemble teeth of file. Tail is prehensile^G.

STANLEY BREEDEN

Where found: Coastal wetlands in northern Aust.

Habits: Can move on land but seldom leaves water. Spends day in shaded water, hunts at night. Anchors itself by its tail, then ambushes passing fish. Lacks venom, so holds prey with help of rough scales and long curved teeth. Several males court a female, who later produces up to 27 young.

Notes: Breathes through nostrils pushed above water, and also through the skin. May move into flooded grassland during Wet season. Harmless to humans.

Status: Secure.

Similar species: Little File Snake, *A. granulatus*, smaller, marked with narrow bands.

* The Arafura Sea bounds the northern coast of Australia.

HABITAT
NORTHERN
WETLANDS

FOOD
FISH

Blackish Blind Snake

Rhamphotyphlops nigrescens (= blackish beaked blind-eye)

Length: HBT to 75 cm

Identification: Wormlike burrowing snake with shiny scales (same size all around body). Eyes are small spots. Small mouth behind and below snout. Upper surface purplish to blackish. Underside cream or pinkish. Very short tail ends in a spine.

IAN MORRIS

Where found: On or in ground in forests, woodlands and plains, in eastern Aust. from southern Qld to Vic.

Habits: On surface of ground only on warm nights, usually after rain. Shelters under rocks, in soil under leaf litter or in deserted termite mounds, sometimes with others of its kind. Eats eggs, larvae and pupae of ants, as well as worms and leeches. Female lays 5–20 eggs in mid to late summer.

Notes: Body suited to burrowing. Glossy scales overlap and head and neck produce oily substance which eases passage through soil. When threatened, may curl with head hidden and lift up tail. Blind snakes are non-venomous and harmless to humans.

Status: Secure.

Similar species: This is the largest blind snake.

HABITAT
IN SOIL,
UNDER LITTER

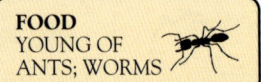

FOOD
YOUNG OF
ANTS; WORMS

Green Tree Snake

Dendrelaphis punctulata (= fine-spotted tree-snake)

Length: HBT to 170 cm

Identification: Slender, tree-living snake with large eyes. Varies greatly in colour, upper surface from pale green to grey-blue to nearly black. Skin between scales is pale blue. Underside may be yellow, lime green or pale blue. Keeled belly scales give a good grip on branches, helped by long, whip-like, prehensile tail.

Where found: Forests, heaths and woodlands, in coastal northern and eastern Aust.

Habits: Lives in trees and other vegetation, shelters in tree hollows, under rocks, in caves and sometimes in buildings. Hunts during day and evening, taking frogs and lizards. Has no venom and is harmless to humans.

Notes: When threatened, lifts the head and flattens the neck sideways, showing blue skin between the scales.

Status: Secure.

Similar species: Northern Tree-snake, *D. calligastra*, has dark streak along side of head and larger eye, is found only in northeastern Qld.

JIRI LOCHMAN

HABITAT
FORESTS &
WOODLANDS

FOOD
FROGS &
REPTILES

Dugite

Pseudonaja affinis (= related false-cobra)

Length: HBT to 200 cm

Identification: Medium to large, fast-moving brown snake with small head. Upper surface brown or brownish grey with black spots. Underside pale grey or brown, with darker blotches. Blackish brown iris, gold rim around pupil. Inside of mouth pink.

Where found: Area around coast of southwestern WA.

Habits: Ground-living snake which is active by day, hunting mammals, lizards and snakes. Alert and nervous, if it feels threatened it rears its forebody, hisses and strikes. In breeding season, males wrestle in combat. Female lays up to 31 eggs in burrow or under rock.

Notes: Dugite and related "brown snakes" have powerful venom, which can be fatal to humans. If bitten, apply elastic bandage to limb and seek immediate medical attention. Antivenom[G] is available.

Status: Secure.

Similar species: Gwardar, *P. nuchalis*, in dry regions to north and east of Dugite. Eastern Brown Snake, *P. textilis*, in eastern, less dry areas of Aust. Bite from either is potentially fatal.

MARIE LOCHMAN

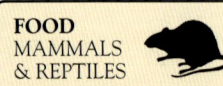

HABITAT SANDPLAIN & HEATH

FOOD MAMMALS & REPTILES

50

Eastern Tiger Snake

Notechis scutatus (= shielded southern snake)

Length: HBT to 210 cm

Identification: Large snake with broad, strong body. Upper surface brown, brown-green or blackish with pale bands. Underside cream, yellow or grey.

Where found: In damp, cool habitats such as swamps, and woodlands on coastal lowlands and plains of southeastern Aust., from southeastern Qld to southeastern SA, and Murray River valley.

Habits: Ground-living snake which is active by day and during warm evenings, hunting frogs, reptiles, nestling birds and fish. Shelters in burrows, in logs and under timber. If threatened, curves the forebody off the ground, flattening it, and hisses loudly. Adult males wrestle. Female has up to 80 live young.

Notes: Shy, but bites if threatened. Venom of this and other related tiger snakes is potentially fatal to humans. Antivenom is available.

Status: Secure.

Similar species: Subspecies known as Western Tiger Snake, *N. s. occidentalis,* occurs in southwestern WA.

HABITAT
SWAMPS,
WOODLANDS

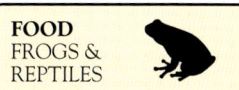

FOOD
FROGS &
REPTILES

Northern Death Adder

Acanthophis praelongus (= very long spine-snake*)

IAN MORRIS

Length: HBT to 70 cm

Identification: Ground-living snake with large head, narrow neck and strong body. Upper surface dark brown to reddish brown, with paler cross-bands. Head scales are rough and form brow-ridges over eyes. Pupil is vertical in daylight. Tail tapers sharply and end bears a spine.

Where found: On loose soil or under leaf litter, in woodland or grassland across northern Aust.

Habits: Shelters under ground litter in shade of rocks or trees during day. Camouflaged by colour, stillness, lies in wait for lizards, frogs, birds and mammals. End of the tail is held near head and acts as a lure to bring prey close.

Notes: Fangs are long and venom is powerful. Warns by flattening body and flicking forebody from side to side. Bite is potentially fatal to humans and requires immediate medical attention.

Status: Probably secure.

Similar species: Southern Death Adder, *A. antarcticus*, in south and southeast of Aust., Desert Death Adder, *A. pyrrhus*, in northwest and Centre.

* Refers to spine at end of tail.

HABITAT
WOODLAND, GRASSLAND

FOOD
REPTILES, FROGS

Stephens's Banded Snake

Hoplocephalus stephensii (= Stephens's armoured-head)

Length: HBT to 125 cm

Identification: Broad-headed, slender-bodied, climbing snake. Upper surface black, with bright yellow scales forming cross-bands two or more scales in width. Yellow spots on head, yellow bars on upper lip. Underside grey, with keeled scales.

Where found: Wooded ranges and rainforest edges, from Gosford, NSW, to southern Qld.

Habits: Lives and shelters in trees. Hunts lizards, small mammals (bats) and birds in tree hollows and crevices in rocks. Female has 2–12 young every second year.

Notes: This snake shelters in scars in tree trunks which only become suitable when tree is mature. Selective timber felling destroys habitat. Bite requires medical assessment.

Status: Rare and endangered.

Similar species: Endangered Broad-headed Snake, *H. bungaroides*, of Sydney area.

HABITAT
MATURE
TREES

FOOD
REPTILES &
MAMMALS

Yellow-faced Whipsnake

Demansia psammophis (= Van Diemen's sand-snake)

Length: HBT to 110 cm

Identification: A slender-bodied, thin-necked, fast-moving snake. Upper surface varies in colour from light grey to reddish, each scale edged darker. Under surface grey to cream. Each large eye is rimmed dark, and forms the head of a "comma" whose tail is a dark marking, bordered yellow, which slants back towards the angle of the mouth.

Where found: In many habitats over most of Aust., except for tropical north from Kimberley Division, WA, to western Qld.

Habits: A day hunter, feeding on small lizards, frogs and reptile eggs. Female lays up to 9 eggs, sometimes in a nest with other females' eggs. It is venomous, though reluctant to bite. Only a very large individual is likely to harm a human, but if bitten seek medical advice.

Notes: Up to 20 adults have been found together in a refuge in cold winter weather.

Status: Common.

Similar species: None.

JIRI LOCHMAN

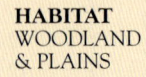
HABITAT
WOODLAND & PLAINS

FOOD
FROGS & LIZARDS

Golden Seasnake

Aipysurus laevis (= smooth high-tail)

Length:
HBT to 170 cm

Identification:
Large, strong-necked, thick-bodied seasnake with paddle-like tail. Upper surface has smooth scales, and varies in colour from dark purple- or green-brown to cream. May have lighter or darker spots on body. Underside has keeled scales and is paler in colour.

Where found: Around tropical coasts and reefs off northern Aust.

Habits: Shelters among or near coral, is active day or night. An individual may be found regularly in one part of a reef. Hunts by probing crevices amongst corals for sleeping fish, prawns, crabs and fish eggs. Female gives birth to 1–5 large young.

Notes: The seasnake most likely to be seen by divers. Will investigate swimmer closely, then swim away. Not usually aggressive. Venom is powerful and potentially fatal to humans. Seek medical assistance if bitten.

Status: Secure.

Similar species: None.

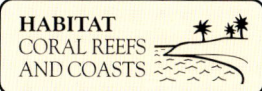

HABITAT
CORAL REEFS
AND COASTS

FOOD
FISH &
MARINE LIFE

Glossary [G]

aestivate. To become inactive in time of drought.

altitude. Height above sea level.

amphibian. Ectothermic vertebrate with moist, non-scaly skin.

antivenom. Substance which counters the effect of venom.

basking. Exposing body to warmth.

camouflage. Colours and patterns which blend with background.

carrion. Dead flesh.

ectothermic. Refers to animal whose body temperature remains close to that of its environment.

extinct. Existing no longer.

fertile. Capable of reproducing itself.

fertilise. Unite female and male cells.

gape. Distance between jaws.

glandular. Containing glands.

habitat. Where an animal or plant lives.

horizontal. Level. Parallel with the horizon line.

introduced. Brought from another place.

irregular. Each part different from other parts. Without regularity or order.

keeled. Bearing a central ridge.

native. Originating in the place or country.

prehensile. Capable of grasping.

range. Geographical area in which an animal or plant occurs.

species. Group of similar animals which, mated, produce fertile offspring.

status. How many of a species exist and whether increasing or decreasing.

subspecies. Further division of a species.

territory. Area claimed by an animal as feeding and/or breeding ground.

toxin. Poison.

tubercle. Small cone-shaped bump.

tympanum. Eardrum formed of membrane, visible in some frogs and reptiles.

venom. Poison of animal origin.

vent. Final opening of digestive tract.

vertebrate. Animal with a backbone.

vertical. Upright. At right angles to the horizon line.

Recommended further reading

BARKER, GRIGG & TYLER, 1995. *A Field Guide to Australian Frogs*. Surrey Beatty & Sons, Sydney.

COGGER, H.G., 1992. *Reptiles & Amphibians of Australia*. Reed, Sydney.

SLATER, P. 2000. *Encyclopedia of Australian Wildlife*. Steve Parish Publishing, Brisbane.

SLATER, P., PARISH, S. 1997. *Amazing Facts About Australian Frogs and Reptiles*. Steve Parish Publishing, Brisbane.

STRAHAN, R. (Ed.) 1992. *Encyclopedia of Australian Animals: Frogs. Reptiles*. Angus & Robertson, Sydney.

PHOTOGRAPHY: Steve Parish (uncredited) and Australia's finest nature photographers Ian Morris, Jiri Lochman, Stanley Breeden, as credited.

ACKNOWLEDGEMENTS: The author's thanks are due to the staff of the Queensland Museum and to designer Leanne Nobilio whose design talent has contributed so much to this series. Audra Colless designed the cover and title page.

First published in Australia by Steve Parish Publishing Pty Ltd
PO Box 1058, Archerfield, Queensland 4108 Australia
www.steveparish.com.au
© copyright Steve Parish Publishing Pty Ltd, 1997
ISBN 1 74021 050 6